The American Mustang

By

Jimmie Dale Brown
August, 2015

An Emery Perry Western Story

WGA Registration Number: 1798139

![Black and white photograph of a valley in the Rocky Mountains of Montana with a pond, rocky terrain, and mountain peaks]

The Valleys of the Rocky Mountains of Montana, The Wild Mustang's Kingdom

- *Our goal is to protect America's wild horses and burros by stopping the federal government's systematic elimination of these national icons from our public lands. It's not too late to act to save the mustangs!*

INTRODUCTION

The year is 1938. Wild horses are being rounded up and sold at packing houses to be killed, cut up, and packed into 50 gallon drums and sent to Europe and Asia for human consumption and to meat packing plants in Portland, Oregon and Chicago, Illinois among other places, to be shipped or ground up into dog food. It was reported that in one year more than 300,000 wild horses were captured and sold to the Portland plant for slaughter.

Move ahead now to the 20th century: A bill was attached by Senator Conrad Burns of Montana, as a rider to the government appropriations bill that would allow wild horses be rounded up for slaughter.

In 1971, Congress passed a law that banned the inhumane treatment of wild horses and put safe guards into place so they couldn't be sold for slaughter. That law was the result of a two-decades-long crusade by Velma Johnston, better known as "Wild Horse Annie." But in December 2004 that law was gutted. Just days before the Thanksgiving holiday recess, when most of Washington was getting ready to leave for the long weekend, Senator Burns put the final touches on his rider No. 142, which removed all protections for wild horses (and burros) that were over the age of 10 or had been offered unsuccessfully for adoption three times. Such animals could now be sold "without limitation, including through auction to the highest bidder, at local sale yards or other convenient livestock selling facilities." Senator Burns inserted his one-page rider into a 3,300-page budget-appropriations bill on the eve of the bill's congressional deadline, and there would be no opportunity for either public or legislative debate.

Equine enthusiasts have been battling land owners and our own government to save the wild mustang for a hundred years and more. The fight has been long and difficult. While most people in this country can't imagine what is happening, there is still wholesale slaughter by slaughterhouses. Some congressmen are still trying to sneak bills into congress to eliminate the wild mustang. The Bureau of Land Management is now actively trying to shut down all instances of horses being sold for slaughter. Cases are still being

identified where their best efforts
are still lacking.

WHITE LIGHTNING,
KING OF THE WILD MUSTANGS

This is a fictional story of one of the survivors. White Lightning is his name and freedom is his aim.

ON A CLEAR DAY IN EASTERN MONTANA

On a clear and blazing day in late May, a white pickup truck jolted along a narrow road through a remote stretch of the semiarid desert of eastern Montana. Though the hillsides burst with fiery yellow and smoky purple wildflowers, the landscape was anything but lush. Dry creek beds shone white confirming that no rain had fallen in months; the soil, upon close inspection, bore more tough shrubs than tender grass or flowers – green rabbit brush and black sage, along with some Indian rice grass and needle-and-thread. "Keep your eyes open," the driver, Jack Boone, told his two passengers. "They could be anywhere." Suddenly the truck bounced over a rise and a band of about a dozen horses – brown, black, gray – became visible. They all looked well-fed and healthy, despite the bleak landscape; several had gangly foals trotting at their sides. "There they are," Boone said. "Look at that white stallion! Isn't he beautiful?" I'll have that beauty or know the reason why." A white stallion, well-muscled, and large for a wild mustang, eyed the truck warily as it approached, then turned and moseyed away. He seemed little concerned, but when Boone and his men left the truck and began to walk toward the horses, he suddenly swung and started toward them. The visitors beat a hasty and undignified retreat. Later, as the truck jolted along another road, a second small band of horses appeared, this time mostly paints. These mustangs didn't wait for a closer look but galloped swiftly away, manes flying, into a valley where a couple of distant pronghorns also could be seen. The bond between human and horse has been the stuff of legend ever since the first intrepid person climbed aboard an equine back. Celebrated in story and song for their beauty, speed and intelligence, horses – especially wild horses – hold a special place in our hearts. But the true picture of wild-horse life in America isn't romantic. It includes, of course, great privations and struggles to exist on the acreage still allotted to the horses. Lately, it also includes the grim image of wild horses being slaughtered and served on dinner plates in Europe, or ground into pet food.   Wild mustangs still roam the vast western plains....ranging right to the foothills of the Rocky Mountains in Montana, and more specifically, right up to Emery Perry's home pasture. Their range is large and is sometimes more rugged than most rocky peaks of any mountain range in North America. But, they've survived and flourished for hundreds of years. The beautiful wild mustang is as swift as its forebears who bore the Spanish Conquistadores on their early conquests. This is a story of the wild mustang, a story of their daily lives, their problems, and their fight for existence. It is no different than that of mankind....an eternal struggle for life, liberty and the pursuit of happiness. They have their young to rear, their families to protect, their enemies to combat....as with mankind, those that use their brain as well as their brawn, are the ones that survive. And foremost among the enemies of the untamed herds, is MAN, who goes forth each year to round them up....

Estimated number of Mustangs by state

State	Horses	Burros	Total	Max. AML
Arizona	303	4,860	5,163	1,676
California	4,395	2,946	7,341	2,200
Colorado	1,415	0	1,415	812
Idaho	633	0	633	617
Montana	172	0	172	120
Nevada	27,599	2,611	30,210	12,811
New Mexico	175	0	175	83
Oregon	4,327	49	4,376	2,715
Utah	4,550	355	4,905	1,956
Wyoming	3,760	0	3,760	3,725
Total	47,329	10,821	58,150	26,715

*Note: Most wild Mustangs are located in the Sierra Nevada Mountains of Eastern California, Nevada, (where most mustangs survive and flourish), Arizona, and in the mountains and plains from New Mexico to Montana with a wild mustang rescue home in Oklahoma.

Chapter 1
MUSTANG ROUNDUP

Dust flies as a large herd of wild mustangs are driven by ten cowboys. There is the sound of thundering hoofs as the mustangs are urged on by the Cowboys who yelp and whistle and wave their lassoes to keep the herd moving. A horse-drawn buckboard moves with the flow. After a long struggle, the riders force the leading front of the herd into a rocky enclosure. Dust swirls as riders jockey for position to control movement of the animals.

On a ridge overlooking the roundup is a man and two boys, dressed in typical cowhand outfits. One of the boys appears to be about ten years old the other a little older, maybe a teenager. They sit on their horses and watch the herd from a ridge a few hundred feet above the valley. They are at a vantage point to see all the action of the roundup.

Hank Keller is in his late sixties, and has a kindness in his face that draws people to him. His sun-drenched skin looks leathery tough under the high-crowned, wide-brimmed black hat. Hank sits on Ginger, Old Hank's favorite. Tommy Fletcher sits on a Pinto next to his guardian. He is nine years old, with a curiosity of two boys his age. A shock of blonde hair pokes from under his white cowboy hat. Tommy has waited all the time he can wait before starting the questions, "What are they doing to those wild mustangs Mister Hank?" Hank has a look like he has been eating green persimmons when he answers, "Every couple of years, Jack Boone and some of the other ranchers raid the herds of wild horses and ship them off to the market. Some are adopted by interested parties, but many are shipped off to the dog food companies, and some are even shipped overseas to countries that market horse meat as food for human consumption." Hank looks at Mateo. I hate it and if there were anything I could legally to stop it, you can bet your hat I would stop it right now. The Department of Land Management says that the land can only support a limited number of the wild mustangs."

ABOVE THE VALLEY IN THE FOOTHILLS
OF THE ROCKY MOUNTAINS

More mustangs, still on the move, are headed to join up with the rest of the herd. On the ridge overlooking the roundup, Hank points to a swarthy looking man of unusual size. Boone appears to be of average height, but is broad across the shoulders and narrow at the waist. Boone is obviously a powerful man physically and a dangerous man to cross. "There's Boone over there. Jack Boone, mid-thirties, mounts his black, saddle horse. Not far away, two Riders urge their mounts on. Tommy looks up at Hank, "Do you ever go on these horse roundups, Mister Hank?" Hank answers definitely, and strongly, "No, Tommy. Me and my men never go on the drives. We feel as if the horses belong here. They've lived here for hundreds of years. The Spanish first brought them to America, and over the years they were released, escaped, or were stolen by Native Americans. This is their home. Here is where they've raised their families." Tommy continues his questions, "Horses have families too?" Hank Keller tries to make Tommy understand. "Why yes… Thomas, of course. Just the same as we do. That's why I sort of feel it's not fair to drive them off like they're doing down there now." "Mister Hank, you called me Thomas again. I told you I haven't liked that name since the accident. My dad called me Thomas. Mom called me Tommy. I like Tommy better. Thomas just seems to bring back bad memories." Hank frowns, and answers, "I'm sorry about that Tommy, Please excuse me if I forget and call you Thomas. I forget sometimes. I remember your father calling you Thomas and it just slips out. Tommy understands what Hank is saying and decides he will not say anything else about it. Old Hank had a sort of hurting look on his face as he explained the name. It's obvious that there is some emotional tie between the boy called Tommy, and Old Hank.

"Hi Sonny." Tommy brightens as he sees the E-P ranch foreman ride up. "Well, I see they've got that big black horse again. They got him last year, and the year before, but he's a pretty clever horse--pretty smart.

"Look Mister Hank, there's Black Fury standing in the stream. See him Sonny?" "Yep, that's him all right. Your Mister Hank can tell you all about him. Tell Tommy the story Hank," Sonny encourages.

"Tell me the story, Mister Hank." Ginger whinnies. "Now, that's alright old girl, that's all right. You and I know Black Fury don't we?" "Ginger?" Tommy asks quickly. "Yeah of course she does. All right, I'll tell you the story." Hank takes a deep breath and settles back against the fence.

"Don't forget to tell him about the little burro." Sonny encourages. "Well now…maybe you should tell him about the little burro, Sonny. The burro was a friend of yours." "What do you mean?" Sonny frowned. "I want to hear about Black Fury." Tommy insists. Old Hank opens up and starts the story of Black Fury. "Well, you see Tommy, Ginger used to be a wild horse, just like Black Fury and the rest of the herd of wild ones being rounded up. Boone and his men caught Black Fury along with the others. That's when they caught the burro. They caught him but when Black Fury escaped, the little burro went with him.""Yep, the little burro followed right behind them," Sonny added. "Nobody even noticed the little burro." Sonny laughs. "Did White Lightning and Black Fury run away together," Tommy asked.

"No sir," Old Hank replied. "You see, Black Fury plays a lone hand. White Lightning came along later.

Pretty soon Black Fury comes across a Pinto and his herd of mares. Black Fury and the big black and white stud begin to fight."

FIGHTING FOR THE HERD

"What happened?" Tommy was wide-eyed. "Just listen—I'm a fixin' to tell you about one of the greatest fights in Wild Mustang history." Old Hank looks off into the distance as if he is seeing the actual fight being relived.

Chapter 2

Black Fury utters a snort, followed by a loud, sharp neigh. Then the Pinto stallion moved forward slowly. There was little difference in the two stallions. Each was a king in his own right. Each was powerful and beautiful to see. Black Fury charges in the direction of the black and white pinto as the Pinto's herd moves away. They approach each other at a full gallop. Then at the moment of contact they both scream in unison, their heads no longer held high, but thrusting trying to get to the others front legs or the head and neck to cripple the opponent. The two stallions bite and kick, rear up, neigh loudly, and do fierce battle. The herd watches to see if the Pinto will win and continue to be their leader, or if Black Fury will take over the herd. The two horses go from being on their knees, to avoid being bitten, to kicking and pawing. Anything to harm their opponent. The fierce battles last for over a minute and a half. Finally, the Pinto signals defeat by running away. "Well, the pinto put up a good fight, but he was no match for Black Fury. Black Fury whipped the pinto and took over his herd." Old Hank laughs. "I reckon he thought he could whip anything."

"Wow, what happened to White Lightning?" Tommy asked. Old Hank clears his throat and hesitates as he gathers his thoughts. "Oh my, that's a long story. But it's no more interesting than what happens to most humans."

EMERY PERRY JOINS THE WATCHERS

As they sit and talk about the great stallions Emery Perry, OWNER OF THE E-P RANCH, rides up. "Now here's the man that can tell you the whole story. I told him and Sonny the story so long ago that I've almost forgotten some of the details. Maybe Emery will tell you boys the story.

"Mateo insists. "Gosh Mister Emery--you've just got to tell us more." Emery yawns and covers his mouth. "It's getting' late Mateo. Tomorrow we'll get up early and while we are going back out to watch the drive, I'll tell you the story of White Lightning." In fact, I hope Hank will let you go with us to follow the roundup. You are old enough to experience the challenges of the roundup. Sonny and I will he headed that way in the morning."

"I think that's a great idea," Hank says. "Okay, Mateo you stay close to me tonight, we will leave early in the morning."

BUNKHOUSE AREA

Some singing cowhands, one strumming a guitar, stand next to the bunk as they continue singing "On Montana Skies". Emery and Mateo walk toward the cowhands as another cowhand, riding a black horse and having another horse in tow, crosses behind their path. Emery and Mateo stand near the cowhands admiring their singing. When the song ends, Emery and Mateo applaud.

Emery says, "That's great boys, fine. I didn't know you could sing that well. How about a song from you, Mateo? Mateo, kicking the dirt, Awwww... I can't sing. Emery disputes that, Oh yes you can. I heard Slim teaching you a song the other day. MATEO (hesitant) Oh... we were only fooling. Emery (patting him on the shoulder), go ahead Mateo... Sing them a song. Mateo pushes his hat back, okay, you asked for it. Let me borrow your guitar," Mateo says, and begins singing and strumming the guitar.

Mateo starts singing "Oh Give Me a Home Where the Buffalo Roam"...After he sings about one verse, he climbs on a saddle that is on a rack. "That's it. I don't know many American cowboy songs. I know many Mexican cowboy songs."

"Hey, how many songs do you know? Me and the boys might be able to join in with you. We know lots of Mexican songs too." "Which ones do you know?" Mateo hesitates as he thinks and says, "Well, I know Salado de Levita, and Cana, and Brava, and La Malaguena…

and…" "Hey wait a minute," the cowhand says. "You know lots more songs than we do, sing one." Mateo sings Solado de Levita. He is near the conclusion of the song when, in the background, there is the clanging of the dinner bell. Mateo doesn't hear the bell and, now into the singing, begins to sing another song. Three of the singing cowboys head for the mess hall. The singing cowhand who was strumming the guitar is anxious for Mateo to end the song so he can go eat as well. Mateo ends the song by turning and pointing a finger where the singing cowhands had been standing. The singing cowhand who owns the guitar grabs his guitar from Mateo and takes off running to the mess hall as Mateo wonders where everybody has gone. Realizing that the dinner bell has rung, he takes off running after the guitar-strumming singing cowhand.

Mateo is in such a hurry he falls down, but he is back on his feet quickly and continues to scurry toward the mess hall.

Tommy struggles to keep up. He is an orphan and has been staying with Old Hank since his parents were killed in an accident up in the Mountains. Old Hank is his Uncle, the brother of Tommy's dad.

Chapter 3

RANCH - MORNING

It's morning and Mateo and the cowboys are up and ready for some action. "Morning, Johnny," Mateo says.

"Morning Mateo," Johnny replies" "Where's Mister Emery?" Mateo asks. "He's over by the barn with Sonny," the cowboy replies. "Shall I saddle Tommy's horse too," Sonny asks. Old Hank turns around. "Oh, you might as well. We'll be leaving soon." "Since you taught him how to cinch his own horse, he wants to do it all himself." Sonny says. Old Hank looks off toward the mountains surrounding the ranch. "You know he's like a maverick...no father...no mother. Seems like a fella should have at least one parent, doesn't it?" Sonny shakes his head, "Pretty tough... but then I guess he's pretty lucky to have a guardian like you to watch after him." "Oh, he goes along without complaining, but sometimes he seems to wonder about some things." "Have you told him the story of his parents," Emery asks. Hank hesitates, "No I haven't. After his parents died I took him in and been the closest thing to a father to him." "I never have heard the whole story," Emery says. Do you have the time?"

"Why not," Hank says. "Listen carefully," Old Hank says. "I don't chew my cabbage twice." Hank starts the story. "It was a day like any other. Kinda nice, you know. It was not a day for dying."

OLD HANK TELLS THE FLETCHER'S TRAGIC STORY

Frank Fletcher was in his mid-thirties, ruggedly handsome, and

Barbara was in her early thirties, and very attractive. When the Fletcher's came to visit, Frank entered the ranch house as normal people would, but suddenly eight-year-old Tommy charged past his parents and stuck his hand out to greet Hank. "I'm Tommy Fletcher and I'm eight years old. I want to learn how to ride a horse." Hank, (shaking Tommy's hand), Well, I'm your dad's older brother, I'm your Uncle Hank and I'm proud to know you.

I turned to Barbara. "Hello Barbara, Frank is lucky he found you before I did. You get more beautiful every time I see you. Barbara gives me a peck on the cheek, "I've missed your little white lies."

Frank smiles, "Since he's ten years older than me, he would've been robbing the cradle." Hank moves to Frank and gives him a bear hug greeting.

I says, "I sure miss you guys since you decided to move back East." "I miss you, too. But, I don't miss the roads." Frank returned. "Yeah, they're just wagon paths. My old truck rides those roads rougher than a buckboard."

About that time someone knocked hard n the door. I moved to the front door and opened it. Pete, one of our cowhands, entered, loaded down with baggage. Frank stepped forward and says, "Here, let me help you." He took some of the suitcases from Pete. I told Pete and Frank to just put their stuff in the room at the top of the stairs. Pete looked at the staircase and frowned. Then he headed up the stairs with the suitcases he still had in his hands. Frank looking around said, "Ah, this place brings back some good memories." "You should come more often. I haven't seen Tommy since he was a baby. That's been a long piece of time."

Barbara spoke up and said, "You'll have to come to Pennsylvania and visit us." I let them know right away that I don't get that far from this ranch, "I don't know...I've never been one for long train rides." Tommy was getting bored with adult talk, and headed for the door. "I'm gonna visit the horses."

MORNING

BREAKFAST AT THE SIERRA PINES RANCH

Me and Tommy, Frank, and Barbara enjoyed breakfast together. Rosetta is our ranch cook, and about that time she enters with a coffee pot. "More coffee?" I point to my cup and says "Don't mind if I do." Barbara declines and says, "I'm so full I couldn't eat or drink another thing." Rosetta fills my cup, and then heads back to the kitchen.

"I'm not thrilled about you two city slickers wandering around the mountains for a week. I'd hate to lose my only brother and sister-in-law." Frank replies, "It has to be done. That's how we make our living... taking photographs of beautiful places." "We'll be fine. We've been in wilder places in Central and South America." Frank brings up "Shorty" Watson. "I was told that "Shorty" Watson knows these mountains better than anyone. He'll keep us safe."

I agreed with Frank, "Yeah, Shorty is the best guide around. You two be careful and smiling I said, "Well, we'll do what we can to keep Tommy occupied."

EASTERN ROCKY MOUNTAINS - DAY

Frank, Barbara, and Shorty Watson set up camp in the snow country. A burro and three horses were tied to a line nearby. A waterfall roared in the distance. Oh, they had picked a pretty spot all right, but a dangerous one. More than they realized. Frank picked up a bag and a camera on a folded tripod, and turned to his two companions, "Everybody ready?"

Barbara and Shorty picked up their bags and they moved toward the sound of the falls.

Hank stops and takes a deep breath as he tells the story of Tommy's parents. It's apparent that he is getting emotional with the telling of the painful story. "Now you do realize I'm piecing this story together from what we know and what we just surmise?"

"Right, Emery says. Go ahead."

"Well, okay. Frank had his camera on the tripod set up on a rock ledge overlooking the falls. Shorty was concerned and told Barbara that where Frank is located is not a safe place for him to be.

Barbara says to Frank, "FRANK... SHORTY THINKS YOU NEED TO GET OFF THAT LEDGE!" Frank points at the falls and shakes his head to indicate he can't hear her over the roar of the water. She moved to where he is looking through the camera.

Barbara shouted, "FRANK! SHORTY SAYS THIS IS NOT A SAFE SPOT!" There was a loud cracking sound. The ledge begins to give way. Barbara reaches out to grab Frank's hand. She succeeds, and the camera tumbles to the river hundreds of feet below. Frank screamed, "LET GO! SAVE YOURSELF!" By instinct, she hangs on.

Shorty grabs a rope, but it is too late. The ledge gives way taking Frank and Barbara with it. Shorty looked down at the river, but there was no sign of Frank and Barbara.

Old Hank holds his head with his hands and SOBS.

LATER

"That boy can sure ask a lot of questions" Sonny laughs about Tommy, "but he's like all little boys I guess." Old Hank came into the room, "It is hard living out here with us old fellas with no kids to play with---I guess city folks see more and learn quicker."

"I don't know about that," Sonny replies. "Seems to me nature hands down the same rules for all of us. Kinda universal. It makes no difference where we live." "I reckon you're right. Here comes Mateo," Sonny points out.

Old Hank looks around to see that Tommy is not in the room. "I reckon Tommy is sleeping in. He does that sometimes when he's especially tired. He's not very strong. He'll probably be mad at me for not getting him up, but I think the little feller needs the rest."

Mateo comes into the room, ready to go. He's still chewing his breakfast.

"Morning Mateo." "Morning Mister Emery. Morning Sonny. See, I got up early. I'm ready to hear the story of White Lightning and Black Fury." "Fine," Emery said. "Let's get cinched up and get started. We've got a lot to do."

A WHINNY COMES FROM WHITE LIGHTNING

Old Hank is talking to White Lightning, "Oh hello old friend. Did you think I had forgotten you? No old sidekick...this is your day to run. We're going right up to the gate. This is your holiday White Lightning." Emery Walks to the gate. "You see Mateo, how he knows right where the gate is. Now, stay back Mateo." There you are White Lightning. It's time for you to go on your run." "Won't he run away, Mister Emery?" Emery smiles: "No, hasn't run away yet." "Why do you turn him out every day like this," Mateo asks. Emery smiles, "Oh, I made a bargain with him a long time ago." "How can you make a bargain with a horse?" Mateo frowns.

"Mateo, after I've told you the story of White Lightning you'll understand how it is that sometimes horses are like people, with the same problems." Emery opens the gate, "There you are White Lightning… have your run." "Why aren't you riding White Lightning today?" Mateo asks. "Oh, I rode White Lightning pretty hard yesterday, so today is his holiday to do as he pleases. He'll stay near by. Come on, let's get started. You know there'll be plenty to do over at the drive. We'll continue on the story of Black Fury and White Lightning while we ride." Hank said. "While Black Fury was stealing the Pinto's mares and becoming the leader of that herd, sort of setting himself up as a king, White Lightning went back to pick up what Black Fury had left of the Pinto's herd, and set out to find a new home and water for <u>his</u> new charges."

"Yeah, and the burro went along too." Sonny reminded. Emery smiles. "That's right Mateo, and White Lightning takes the whole bunch to a place where he figured they could live in peace and contentment. Sorta enjoy the freedom of their new found home where White Lightning watched over his herd."

Chapter 4

Then one day the enemy Jack Boone discovered them." Emery continues. "It was Boone that tracked White Lightning from the roundup where White Lightning had made his escape. White Lightning had to act quickly. He found a way to outwit him. He let Boone see him and he led him away on a long hard chase so that the herd and the mares could make good in their escape. He then, later, led the herd to safety to a new land, a land of enchantment. Where it was peaceful, where there was a big lake. This was far from the beaten path of man. Things were going along well until they were seriously threatened by their worst enemy.

"Boone!" Mateo exclaimed.

"That's right, Mateo. Boone tracked them down again. "Tell me about it Mateo exclaimed." "Okay," Emery said.

Sonny and I were doing some riding, watching for White Lightning when a part of the story happened that makes me get a bad taste in my mouth. Boone and I had a little set to. It wasn't pleasant, but let me begin at the beginning of the trip through the mountains.

We were moving at a slow pace through a forest of aspens. My dog, Sarge, stayed close to us, but occasionally he would take off and chase a rabbit. Sonny was leading a burden-laden pack burro. We were planning to camp and fish for a few days and see if we could catch a glimpse of White Lightning and his herd. It was an absolutely gorgeous day. A snow-capped mountain could be seen through the trees. I told Sonny,

"No matter how many times I come up here, I am awed by the beauty of this place." Sonny agreed, "Yes sir... sure is pretty. What makes you think White Lightning would come this high with his herd?" "Because there's a lush valley just over the rise and this is the only way in coming from the west." Sonny and I were dressed in gear to ward off the cold. We rode into a mountain pass that was covered with snow. The air was so cold we could see our own breath."

I moved forward as Sonny encouraged his mount as we began our descent. We could see a valley with a blue lake below. The lake, fed by several streams, featured one with a waterfall cascading into the lake below.

"There she is Sonny... Blue Bird Valley." "You think White Lightning is down there?" I smiled at Sonny, "I'd bet my ranch on it."

We shed our heavy coats now that we have descended several thousand feet. Before us was a horse's paradise. The valley floor has huge patches of sweet clover and bee flower. Red rock windows, fins, and spires. It was a beautiful valley." "Sonny was taken with the beauty. "I've never seen anything like that before." I had been here before and was familiar with the flora and fauna. "You'd think that this place would be settled." Sonny commented. I told him that at one time the people who occupied this valley were hunters and gatherers. They belonged to one of the Paiute tribes. I told him that Mormons tried settling here. After a while they packed up and left too. It was too far from a community, and very cold in the winters.

I was riding next to a red wall of sedimentary rock. Suddenly, Sonny pulled up and signaled for me to do likewise. Sonny backed up his big Bay. I didn't see anything. Sonny said with a low voice, "White Lightning... Up on a ridge. No more than five hundred yards. White Lightning stood majestic looking. Every bit like a king overseeing his kingdom. He looked around, pawing the ground. Sonny and I dismounted. We held the reins of our mounts as we peeked around the rock.

Suddenly, with a loud NEIGH, White Lightning takes off at a full gallop. Three riders appear, ropes ready. White Lightning made several sharp turns as he eluded the pursuer's lassoes. The men split and continue riding hard. One of the riders cuts

White Lightning off and forced him back toward the other riders. Lassos ready, they cast their ropes and caught White Lightning around the neck. That great white horse put up a fierce fight. But, one of the riders jumped off his horse and wrapped one end of the rope around a live oak. White Lightning charged the dismounted rider, and he dropped his rope and ran for all he was worth. Despite the third rider pulling with all his might, White Lightning yanks the rope out of his hand.

White Lightning galloped in a circle around the tree. When the rope became taut, the friction on the rough bark of the oak severed the rope. White Lightning was free. He neighed as if to mock the hunters. Then he turned and galloped toward a cliff overlooking the lake. Boone's riders were again on their mounts and they take up the chase. When White Lightning reached the edge, he hesitated as he looks back at his pursuers, then jumps into the lake, fifty feet below. White Lightning hit with a tremendous splash. The riders stopped at the edge of the cliff, shook their heads, turned, and rode slowly away.

"So Boone and his riders couldn't capture White Lighting could they," Mateo said. "Not this time," Emery replied, "but he wouldn't give up for a long time." "Now we'd better move along if we're going to get where we're supposed to be today."

"I'm sure glad White Lightning got away."

Chapter 5

"That's right, Mateo, but Boone found White Lightning's tracks and located his new home near the lake." "But he didn't catch him did he?" Mateo exclaimed. Emery frowned at Mateo, and then smiled. "Now Mateo don't get ahead of the story. Boone and his crew did build a trap later, but White Lightning was too smart. You see White Lightning had had a lot of trouble with Boone, and he was always on the alert ready to protect his herd. One day White Lightning came to the vicinity of Boone's trap."

"And the burro would tag along too, wouldn't he Emery?" Sonny interjected. "Yes, Emery replied, "Whenever the herd went anywhere the burro was always there. He was a special friend of White Lightning."

White Lightning, the burro, and the herd were inseparable."

THE LITTLE BURRO WAS A FRIEND
TO WHITE LIGHTNING

"Did Boone trap any of the herd?" Mateo asked. "Ah ha...you're getting' ahead of me again. The little burro did get caught in one of the traps

Boone had prepared. Boone quickly arrived and he and his men put ropes on the burro. White Lightning watched and charged.

White Lightning rescued the burro from Boone and moved his herd quickly away to safety. "White Lightning sure is tough, Mister Emery. I'm glad he's my friend, aren't you?" "Yes, Mateo...he's a great one to have for a friend." Emery answered. "But the danger wasn't over, was it Emery," Sonny said. "There are all kinds of dangers for a wild horse herd just like there are for us if we become careless."

"Right Sonny. That's when White Lightning saw the outlaw, Black Fury. The Outlaw proceeded to kidnap White Lightning's mate. The little fella followed to be near his mother." The pinto followed the black. The colt followed them.

"Black Fury didn't want the colt and chased him away while White Lightning was searching for his mate. She had escaped and gone back to the herd…but the colt was still lost in the wilderness." The colt wanders as White Lightning searches for him. Wolves are howling. A large pack of wolves are looking for a small or weak horse to attack and fill their bellies. White Lightning hears them and hurries to protect the colt. The wolves are attacking the colt when White Lightning comes to the rescue and chases them off.

"Well, the colt was pretty scared. You can't blame him. A hungry pack of wolves chasing you is no fun." Mateo shakes his head in agreement.

"Right, White Lightning had a lot of trouble with Boone and Black Fury, and the wolves and all." Mateo shuddered. "His troubles were just beginning," Sonny said. "You wait 'til you grow up and you'll find out— troubles always come in bunches." "Gosh, it's almost like White Lightning was a human being with a family and all." "That's right, Mateo. I guess they have difficulties with family squabbles and such, just like us folks." Emery answered.

"Just wait 'til you grow up and have a family of your own." Sonny joined in. "I don't think I'll ever get married," Mateo says seriously. "It seems to only lead to trouble and heartache."

Sonny laughs. "Oh no…just wait 'til you grow up and find how sweet it

is to make up." "Look Mister Emery--
Sonny's crying." Mateo says softly.

Mister Emery laughing: "So
would you if you were eating the same
kind of apples he's eating." "Oh, I
like onions, but apples don't agree
with me no how." Sonny says through
his onion induced tears.

Chapter 6

Tell him what happens next--how the family got together again." Sonny encourages. Emery continues: "Well, after White Lightning had driven off the wolves, White Lightning and the little colt went on through the night and returned to the herd, but White Lightning wasn't pleased that his mare had run off with Black Fury-and seeing this the little colt detected that there was discord in the family, and decided to do something about it."

"And you know the old saying "A little child shall lead them." Well, here it is." Sonny said. The little colt goes to White Lightning, then to the mare. The colt calls for White Lightning, and the two horses make up. "Go ahead, Emery. Let's hear the rest of the story." "Okay, okay, Sonny. I'm gettin' there. About the time the little colt had brought peace in the family, Black Fury came back." Black Fury came in pawing the ground and challenging White Lightning.

"This time White Lightning decided to have it out with the black horse—once and for all. So they prepared to do battle to determine who was king of the range. White Lightning and Black Fury Are having a winner take all fight while the little burro is sitting under the tree watching..."Hee Haw"—and the colt watches along with the little burro.

Jack Boone shows up!

Boone turns to his men. "I got me an idea—no sense trying to rope them down there—you fire this rim and I'll get the other. Smoke 'em out and we'll catch them as they come runnin' out."

"Okay!" His partners echo. It is only a few minutes before the fire is spreading. Horses stop fighting, and run in a panic. There is fire all around them, threatening to burn them alive. There is lots of smoke and fire. We hear "Hee Haw", Hee Haw, and we see the little burro leading White Lightning, the herd, and Black Fury through an opening.

Boone and his men are following.

"Did the colt get burned up?" Mateo asked excitedly. "No--no! Two days later the colt wandered into the corral at the ranch and Sonny doctored the colt where he had been burned on the left front leg. White Lightning and the Pinto are both watching from a distance. "That's right," Emery said. "Sonny saw that White Lightning and the colt's mother were watching him so he decided to get out of the way to see what they would do. The mare came into the corral to be near the colt just like any mother would. It's only minutes before the mare and the colt are together. Sonny leaves the gate open and walks away. White Lightning was more skeptical—it took him a little longer to decide just what he wanted to do about it. White Lightning went back and forth and finally enters the gate and joins the mother and colt.

"He'd had an awful hard time out there in the country. That's why I made the bargain to let him run wild and free every day if he'd promise not to run away. You see Mateo, it pays to always keep your promises." "Then what happened to Black Fury," Mateo wanted to know.

Chapter 7

BACK TO THE ROUNDUP

"Well, he's still a wild horse, and in this year's drive, they caught him again." "Look!" Mateo cried excitedly. "There's Black Fury now." Mateo yells as the horses go by below them. Black Fury is being chased by Boone and his men. They rope him, but he breaks loose." "That's the way it always happens," Emery smiled. "I wonder how they expect to hold that horse. Black Fury is loose again somewhere out on the range—out in the wild horse country there's another drama starting. Somewhere out there a large band of wild horses being rounded up. Black Fury is with his herd as usual."

BACK TO THE STORY

"Gee, Mister Emery, I'm sure glad White Lightning is safe now." Emery put his arm around Mateo's shoulder. "Oh, I don't think White Lightning would be scared because he's learned there's more contentment in and ordered, civilized life than to be running wild. You know, a lot of people could take a lesson from White Lightning because after all, he's a wild horse at heart, but he's satisfied. "He's satisfied to be guided by good and gentle influences."

SEMI-DESERT – DAY

Emery, Mateo, and Sonny are riding the hills with White Lightning following." They get off of their horses and scan the area ahead. A number of mustangs are grazing as White Lightning gallops up and joins them. Emery says, "He'll stay nearby. Come on, let's get started. You know there'll be plenty to do over at the drive. Emery and Sonny mount their horses. "Let's go over and see how we can help." The three ride along side-by-side. Mateo is in the middle. C'mon Mister Emery continue with the story of Black Fury and White Lightning. Did the Pinto stay around to try to steal his herd back?" "No, Black Fury stole the Pinto's mares and became leader of the herd... sort of setting himself up as king. You remember we said that White Lightning went back to pick up what was left of his herd and set out to find a new home and water." Let me think, I'll get it right in a moment." Emery tries to remember his flashback of the story of the great horses.

Emery continues the story. "White Lightning looked around majestically. It was really something how White Lightning looked with the wind blowing his mane." He was standing in the middle of a pond as the little burro was rolling in the water. White Lightning neighs and the herd, understanding the signal, moves out as they follow him. White Lightning takes off at a full gallop kicking up dust.

Mateo is excited and asks for more stories. Emery hesitates and picks up the story. "They roamed the West toward the foothills of the great mountains where they found water" Sonny spoke us, "The burro, he went along too." Emery shakes his head, "That's right, Mateo we have time for a little more."

"White Lightning stands guard. He neighs and the mares that make up his herd follow his lead as he moves out. The burro continues to follow along. Now, White Lightning could have lived here with peace and contentment. Sort of enjoy the freedom of their new found home. White Lightning watched over his herd." But, Boone showed up again. That man would not give up. He wanted White Lightning with a passion of a man that was accustomed to getting what he wanted.

Boone rode up and stopped on a rise. He discovered the herd grazing in the valley. It was Boone that tracked White Lightning from the round up where he had made his escape. Boone made his move and started toward the herd. Emery hesitated then continues. "White Lightning had to act quickly he sees Boone and his men about to charge down to the valley where the herd occupied and lived. Most of the herd is in the water drinking and staying cool. White Lightning neighs as a danger signal. The herd moves out quickly." Emery continues, "White Lightning found a way to outwit Boone. White Lightning takes off and Boone charges after him." Mateo says, "Did Boone catch him?" Emery says, "No, He let Boone see him and then he led him away on a long, hard chase so that the herd and the mares could make their escape. Boone and his men rode hard in an attempt to catch White Lightning. Boone finally pulled up near a fallen tree, and looked for a long pause in the direction that White Lightning had taken, and then gives up the chase."

"Not this time, "Boone mutters. "But I will have you someday. I guarantee it.

Chapter 8
WHITE LIGHTNING
KEEPS THE HERD MOVING

"White Lightning leads his mustangs at a full gallop away from danger to a lake surrounded by woods. He then led the herd to safety away from Boone. White Lightning keeps them headed to the North, to a land of enchantment, where he knows of another big lake. The herd enjoyed the peace and tranquility of the new home around the lake." Emery stops and says, "This was far from the beaten path of man. The herd stayed next to the lake in a peaceful setting. They spent the time playing, running and enjoying the perfect life for a herd of mustangs. White Lightning could be seen on a high rise standing majestically watching his herd."

"That sounds wonderful," Mateo says. Emery agrees, "There in the peaceful beauty of the new home, White Lightning began to think of romance." Sonny breaks in, "You're going to like this, Mateo." Emery (tongue in cheek) says, "Oh, shucks. Boys don't like that love stuff much... Sonny smiles, "I know. But it brought a big change in White Lightning's life." Emery agrees, "Kind of like his first step toward his ultimate destiny. White Lightning sees his favorite, American Beauty standing alone, he moves toward her. The little burro is taking all this in as he sits on his rump in the shade of a big oak tree. American Beauty and White Lightning are together as the burro continues to watch. White Lightning nuzzles American Beauty. The little Burro brays. "Sonny observes, "White

Lightning's pal, the burro, got a big kick out of it. You know love is the same in any language." Emery laughs, "They liked each other. That helps." "You ought to know." Sonny says.

"Go ahead with your story." Mateo begs." Emery smiles, "Well Mateo, there isn't much you can say about love. White Lightning picked a fine-looking mare for his mate." The Burro brays his approval of White Lightning's choice."

MONTHS LATER

"We'll jump ahead almost a year." Emery begins his story again. "Then one day there was a new member added to White Lightning's family. White Lightning and American Beauty watch after the new colt." "I'll bet it was a beautiful colt," Mateo says. "I sure wish I could have seen him."

Emery Agrees, "As fine a new colt as was ever born to a mare."

The Burro continues to sit, apparently watching White Lightning and his family. The new colt would look up at his parents in a worshipful attitude. White Lightning and American Beauty stay together. White Lightning would neigh if his little son started to wander.

White Lightning and American Beauty stood near the little Colt, who is still lying on the ground. The burro continues to sit and watch. White Lightning and his mate begin to move. The Colt gets up and moves with them. The Burro rises and follows. The colt stands and nuzzles his mother. He is wanting some dinner.

The Little Colt

Emery says, "White Lightning was proud of his young son. He taught him all the lore of the range. He raised him so that one day he would be strong and brave and smart enough to take care of himself. Yes, and maybe become leader of the herd like his daddy." Emery chuckles.

"The Colt walks up to the water where White Lightning is standing in the middle of the shallow lake. The colt moves slowly out to join him. A snake swims toward the young colt. White Lightning's head pops up as he sees danger is near. The snake continues moving toward he colt, White Lightning's son. White Lightning makes his move. The proud father erupts into a killing frenzy to protect his family. He stomps the snake until there is virtually nothing left of the ugly serpent." Emery comments, "When there was danger, White Lightning would be there to protect his young'un." American Beauty and the Burro watched from the lakeside. Seeing the snake has been killed, the Burro brays numerous times."

White Lightning is walking along the lake with the colt following. American Beauty is watching from near the lake. The colt nuzzles White Lightning."

"You are a good story teller,
Emery. "Is everything you're telling
us the truth. Did it really happen
just that way?" Emery smiles a
mischievous smile and says, "You can
bet a hat on it." Mateo looks at Sonny
for verification and sees Sonny
smiling and shaking his head.

"Go on Mister Emery," Mateo urges.
"I want to hear the rest of the story-
-true or not." Emery continues where
he had left off. "The little fella
could see how White Lightning was
looking after him and protecting him,
and he would try to treat his daddy in
the way little colts have of showing
their affection."

American Beauty and the Colt were
standing near the lake when White
Lightning moves to them and nips at
his favorite playfully, the Burro
watches and sits. There is almost

always a peaceful scene of White Lightning, American Beauty, and the colt standing near the lake.

Chapter 9

PEACEFUL LAKE IN A WOODED AREA

"White Lightning's herd can almost always be seen peacefully grazing in the wooded area around the lake." Emery hesitates and takes a breath. "Are you sure you want me to continue?" "Please," Mateo said. "Go on." "Okay you asked for it. Just tell me if it gets too boring. For a spell the herd lived in quiet and contentment. The colt continued to grow into a fine young horse. But, there were still many things that White Lightning had to teach him. Like the day the little fella got frightened by some cottontail rabbits." Emery chuckles, "Of course, they wouldn't harm a soul. But White Lightning had to show that to his son." White Lighting nudged the colt toward the rabbits. Two cottontail rabbits are eating clover, the rabbit's favorite food. The colt, being scared of the rabbits, moves to his parents. White Lightning moves toward the rabbits, and wants his family to follow. He reaches the rabbits and pokes his nose around them, and then he looks back at the colt to make a point. The colt stands near his mother watching White Lightning and the rabbits. White Lightning shakes his head as to say, "Come on, they won't hurt you," and then moves away. The colt moves away from his mother, and stands stiff legged with a rabbit nearby ready to run if the rabbit charges. The rabbit hops over to the colt. The colt sticks his head down like White Lightning did earlier. The colt moves away from the rabbits, his fears now conquered."

LAKE AREA - NIGHT

"Once, at night," Emery continues, "The colt wandered away from the herd... and got lost. The Colt is alone, and he is frightened." Emery is still making the story up as he goes along, but he can see that Mateo is still interested and enjoying it. Sonny was too! Emery smiles to himself and continues with the story just as it had been told to him by Old Hank Keller. And, what he couldn't remember, he made up.

"The colt is frightened as he strays out alone in the darkness. The Colt walks alone in the darkness. The hoot of an owl is heard. The colt moves in the darkness. The owl hoots again. The colt realizes that darkness surrounds him, and just like humans he is frightened of those things he can't see. White Lightning is moving in the darkness searching for his son." Emery stops to see the reactions of the listeners, and then continues, "But White Lightning went out to search for him and brought him back safely to his mother." White Lightning, American Beauty, and the Colt are together again."

"This happiness White Lightning and his herd had found was destined to be rudely shattered."

The story ends for now as Emery, Sonny, and Mateo continue toward the roundup area.

"Don't stop now, Mister Emery, it's just getting good." Emery laughs, and says, "You really do like stories of wild horses, don't you." Mateo says, "I could listen to stories about the wild mustang forever." Emery looks at Sonny. "You know about as much as I do about White Lightning's story. Old

Hank told you the same stories he told me. You take over." "Okay boss, if you insist. I'm like Mateo. I could listen to wild mustang stories all day and all night. Anyway here goes."

Chapter 10

SONNY CONTINUES THE STORY

"Jack Boone saw White Lightning's tracks and located his new home near the lake." Mateo is concerned, "He didn't catch him, did he?" Sonny admonishes Mateo. "Now, don't get ahead of our story, boy." Sonny has to regain his thoughts. He paused then continued. "Boone did dig a pit trap hoping that White Lightning would get into it and then be captured," Sonny laughs. What's so funny about that Mister Sonny?" Mateo says. Sonny replies, "You'll find out, son." Mateo is concerned, "You gonna tell me, Mister Sonny?" Yep, he did build a trap for him, ah... but White Lightning was too smart. You see, White Lightning had an awful lot of trouble with Boone, and he was always on the alert... ready to protect his herd from the man who had given them so much trouble. White Lightning's herd was grazing below a huge mesa one day when White Lightning brought his herd to the vicinity of Boone's traps." Emery breaks in to remind Sonny, "The burro would tag along too." "Yeah, that's right." Sonny chuckles, "Where ever the herd went...anywhere the herd went, that little burro was always there guarding, listening, and always watching, oh yeah, and sitting." Sonny laughs. "I can just see White Lightning watching his herd, and the Burro following the herd. Well, one day, as the odds would finally play out; White Lightning locates one of Boone's pits and wisely moves away. He moves away with the burro lagging behind. The Burro continues to get farther and farther behind. White

Lightning sees his little friends and issues a loud neigh telling him to catch up with the herd, but White Lightning and the herd keep moving." "What happened," Mateo asks. "Did Boone catch the burro?"

"Sure enough, the burro falls into Boone's trap. The Burro tries to get out, but cannot. White Lightning is with the herd but he hears the burro braying. The burro in the pit continues to bray as a danger signal to White Lightning as he signals for help. White Lightning leaves the herd to help his little friend. He knows that the burro has saved the herd by following, and watching. The little burro seemed to have a peculiar sense for danger, but this time he didn't see the trap until he fell into it. The trapped Burro continues to bray.

White Lightning galloping to the pit. When White Lightning arrives at the pit, the Burro is moving in circles. White Lightning nods that he understands the situation. The Burro wants out! White Lightning used his right front hoof to paw the ground to indicate where the Burro should be able to get out, but the burro hesitates. He has detected a danger and brays out a warning. White Lightning's head perks up--someone is coming!

Boone and his Segundo head for the pit at a full gallop. White Lightning detects the approaching danger and moves away from the pit. Boone and Rogers, the Segundo, continue galloping toward the pit. White Lightning moves to some brush and trees where he can hide. Boone and Rogers arrive at the pit, dismount, and look down into the pit. White Lightning watches the action with fear for the little burro, but keeping in mind the possible danger to his herd. Rogers tosses a lasso around the Burros neck as White Lightning, helpless, continues to watch.

The two men pull and pull trying to get the Burro out. The Burro puts up a fierce battle against the men's efforts to bring him under control.

White Lightning gallops toward the pit. He has come up with a plan. The Burro sits on its rump and the two frustrated men cannot get him out of the pit. Boone hears a horse coming and turns. White Lightning approaches the men at full gallop. Boone indicates to Rogers to let the burro go and concentrate on White Lightning. They run to mount their horses. Meanwhile, the Burro gets out of the pit where White Lightning had shown him and joins White Lightning. The sudden rush by White Lightning has caused Boone's horse to try to break loose and Boone and Rogers are having trouble mounting their horses because the animals are too excited. While Boone and Rogers continue to try to gain control or their horses, White Lightning and the Burro run away."

Chapter 11

Mateo is excited. "Yaaa, White Lightning rescued the burro and they headed away to safety. I sure would like to have seen that. "What happened then? Did Boone give up and go home?" "No boy, that's not the way it happened at all."

"The herd moved around in the lake--stopping to take an occasional drink. It was a peaceful scene." Sonny says, "But troubles for White Lightning and his herd weren't over. This time the danger comes from a different source. Black Fury arrives and watches the herd from a distance."

Emery cuts in, "Right, Watching the herd was Black Fury. Black Fury runs to the lakeside where American Beauty and the Colt are standing.

Now don't ask me how or why it happened the way it did. One would have to be a wild horse to understand all that went on, but Black Fury proceeded to kidnap American Beauty. Black Fury called and she followed."

Chapter 12

After a long run, Black Fury and American Beauty stop to take a drink. American Beauty moves away from the water, and begins a full out run. Black Fury follows her. American Beauty is in a full gallop but, she can't get away from Black Fury." "What happened to the colt," Mateo asks, "He couldn't keep up with American Beauty or Black Fury." Emery nods. "You're right, the Colt, first hesitates, and then takes after his momma. White Lightning hasn't seen what was going on yet, but senses something is wrong. American Beauty continues to run with Black Fury not far behind. White Lightning spots them and neighs; he then takes off after the three."

The little Colt runs to try to be near his mother. He runs through water, falls down, gets up and continues in an effort to catch American Beauty, but American Beauty and Black Fury move at a fast pace." "Where's White Lightning, Mateo asks. Surely he can catch them."

Sonny picks up the story and continues. "White Lightning charges through the water after his mate and Black Fury, the Burro follows as he struggles to go through the water. Black Fury is now leading at a full gallop. Now here's where is gets confusing for me, Emery says, "American Beauty is following Black Fury! Again, I guess you would have to be a wild mustang to understand. She has two great horses wanting her, and she takes off with Black Fury. The Burro finally makes it out of the lake and sees that American Beauty is still running and is now leading Black Fury again and is at a full gallop. The colt struggles and continues to gallop across the semi-desert, but he is falling farther and farther behind. And, then another strange thing happened. "American Beauty finds a place to rest, and stops running. Black Fury moves to join her. Black Fury and American Beauty check each other out as the colt arrives where Black Fury and his mother have stopped. Black Fury rears up and chases the colt away." Black Fury didn't want the colt near and chased him away. The colt leaves and looks for White Lightning. Black Fury knows that White Lightning will be coming for his son and his mate so he moves to a vantage point to verify the colt has gone. The colt moves across the semi-desert at full gallop. Black Fury heads back to American Beauty.

American Beauty paws the dirt and moves away. Then, SHE KICKS AT HIM!... "Women!" Sonny snorts, "They are all the same. Impossible to understand."

White Lightning is in full gallop as he passes a canyon wall, and continues to gallop past desert trees. Black Fury is following American Beauty through low vegetation. After running away with Black Fury, she now wants nothing to do with him. White Lightning is still at a full gallop. American Beauty gallops up a steep incline. She reaches the top and starts her descent. As she in heading down a sharp incline covered with shale she loses her footing and tumbles down the hillside of rock and sand finally righting herself and shaking her head.

Black Fury climbs the same hill at a gallop, and stops at the top.

American Beauty is on the side of the hill trying to shake the effects of the tumble. Black Fury seems indecisive as he goes back and forth. He senses a great danger in the loose shale. He decides to retrace his steps and go back down the way he came up."

Meanwhile, unknown to Black Fury, White Lightning searches below a canyon wall for his mate". Emery says, "While White Lightning searched unsuccessfully for his mate, she had gone back to the herd after escaping from Black Fury. But the colt was still lost in the wilderness.

White Lightning stands on a high place below the canyon wall looking in all directions for a sign of the Colt or American Beauty. White Lightning stands as patiently as possible, looking for his missing family. He broadens his range and while looking in the distance he continues his search.

He walks slowly as he searches through the low shrub. The Colt is lost. As it becomes dark, he hears wolves howling in the distance. Suddenly a pack of wolves charge through the darkness, howling as they move. Fortunately the colt hears the approaching wolves and realizes there is a danger. The pack charges across the terrain, and the frightened Colt begins to run. The Wolves continue to move rapidly.

Meanwhile, White Lightning is still searching as he moves slowly. He smells for a clue. He raises his head and nods as he hears the howling in the distance. The little colt is running as fast as his little legs will carry him. The wolves continue to run and howl. White Lightning takes off in the direction of the howling. By now, the colt realizes he is running for his life. The pack is still at top speed--howling as it moves. White Lightning thunders in the direction of the Wolves.

The colt runs into a problem. The Colt stops quickly as he has run to a dead end. The pack approaches as they howl, and are attacking the young Colt as they have him trapped. He tries to find a way of escape as they snap at his hoofs. The terrified Colt falls down as he tries to escape, but is quickly able to get up. White Lightning is almost there. The howling continues as the Wolves snap at the Colt. The cold tries to kick the wolves, but to no avail. White Lightning comes upon the scene and moves right in the middle of the Wolves. One of the Wolves snaps at

White Lightning. White Lightning rears up and stomps at the Wolves. White Lightning's hoofs come down again and again and finally scatter the Wolves. A wolf tries again and snaps at White Lightning and White Lightning continues to stomp on the Wolves. Finally, the Wolves run off in defeat; howling as they leave. White Lightning leads the colt up an incline and away from the battle scene"

"Wow that was close. White Lightning destroyed a whole pack of wolves!" Mateo says, "The little colt must have been awfully scared."

"Time for a break," Emery says as he dismounts and looks for a shade. Emery now sits, leaning against a tree, with a pipe in his hand. Sonny and Mateo are sitting next to him. Emery says, "Well... pretty scared. You can't blame him. It's no fun to have a pack of hungry wolves chasing you. If not for Boone the wild mustangs wouldn't be in for so much trouble." Mateo says. "Right," Sonny says, "White Lightning had a lot of trouble with Boone and Black Fury, and the Wolves."

Sonny continues, "But, his troubles were only beginning. You wait 'til you grow up and you'll find out. Trouble always comes in bunches." Mateo shakes his head, "Gosh, it's almost like White Lightning was a human being with a family."

Emery agrees, "Yes, Mateo. I guess they have difficulties and family squabbles"...Emery chuckles... "Just like us folks." Sonny tries to give some wise advice, "Just wait 'til you grow up and get married and have a family of problems too.

Mateo contemplating, "I don't think I'll ever get married." Sonny laughs, "Wait'll you see how sweet it is to make up." There's a pause, and then Mateo makes the same request he has been making all day. "Tell him what happened next... How does White Lightning's family got together again." Emery starts again, "Well, after White Lightning had driven off the wolves, he and the little colt went on through the night and arrived at the camp. White Lightning wasn't pleased that his mare had run off with Black Fury. So the little colt, seeing that there was discord in the family, decided to do something about it." Emery helps Mateo down the slope toward where the horses were left.

Chapter 13

Sonny continues the story, "And you know the old saying, "A little child shall lead them." Well, here it is." Emery and the two trail partners get down to the horses. Emery says, "Come on, boys. I'll continue the story while we ride."

"The herd is together in a peaceful setting, except for White Lightning and American Beauty." American Beauty stands by herself, and watches White Lighting. White Lightning is trying to ignore her and, stops at a tree and scratches on the rough bark. American Beauty looks at White Lightning in the distance and neighs. White Lightning is still angry with American Beauty and does not react. She neighs again and waits for a response. There is none. The colt sees what is happening to his family and decides to take a hand. "The Colt moves to White Lightning and American Beauty neighs to her colt thinking the colt was choosing his father over her. The colt then heads back to his mom. The two horses are about a hundred feet apart. American Beauty waits for the colt to return. The colt returns and moves to nurse. Now, White Lightning watches at a distance, shaking his head up and down. The colt sees what White Lightning is doing and leaves American Beauty. He trots to a position halfway between his parents, and waits.

White Lightning hesitates, and then moves toward the Colt. The Burro watches the peace-making efforts of the colt, and from a distance he sees White Lightning continue moving toward the colt. American Beauty hesitates, and then moves toward the colt and

White Lightning. The Burro sits down. White Lightning, American Beauty, and the colt are together again. The Burro is still sitting on its rump. He nods his head and appears to be happy again. He takes a nap.

White Lightning nuzzles American Beauty as if to say, "All is forgiven." The Burro, now standing, brays."

Chapter 14

Emery pauses and starts again, "Then, about the time the little colt had brought peace in the family, Black Fury came back. Black Fury stands majestically shaking his head up and down. He neighs a challenge, White Lightning neighs an acceptance. They move toward each other at a full gallop. This time White Lightning decided to have it out with the black horse, once and for all. They prepared to do battle to prove who was king of the range. White Lightning moves his on looking herd away from the battle arena. This appears to be a showdown similar to the one earlier between White Lightning and the Pinto. White Lightning and Black Fury BITE, STOMP, and KICK each other. The herd and the Burro watch. After nearly three minutes of intense fighting by the great stallions, Boone and Rogers came upon the scene and dismount to watch." "Boone again! Mateo exclaims. Won't that man ever give up?"

Jack Boone says, "Rogers, I've got an idea. There's no sense trying to rope them down in there. Boone points to an area near the battling mustang stallions. You fire that rim and I'll take care of this one. Force'em to the gap and we'll catch them as they come out." Rogers is not sure he likes the idea, but goes along with his boss. "Okay." He mutters.

A SHORT TIME LATER

The two mustangs are still at it as Boone and Rogers start fires at opposite ends of the canyon. Sensing the fire, the herd takes off in a run. Black Fury and White Lightning stop their battle and join in the dash to avoid the flames. White Lightning leads the way as Black Fury, the Colt, and the rest of the herd follow. The flames trap them and the herd stops. Black Fury challenges the fire by stomping, as does White Lightning. Rogers dismounts and sets another fire, then remounts and makes a run for the gap. The horses, surrounded by flames and smoke are confused. They nervously move back and forth. They run from one end of the small canyon to the other. They seem trapped with no way of escape. The Colt is frightened, and separated from his parents. Then, the burro senses an opening brays for the herd to follow him. He leads them to an opening and freedom. The Colt still appears trapped."

Emery, Sonny, and Mateo pause their horses. Mateo can't wait to see what happens to the colt, White

Lightning, Black Fury and the herd. "Did the colt get burned up?" "No" Emery says ... "Two days later he wandered into the south corral at the ranch and you know old Pete, he doctored the colt's burnt leg and it healed up in no time".

Pete, the foreman, is an older gent, and is on his knees applying medicine to the Colt's leg." "What happened then," Mateo asked, Emery continued the story. "Well, overlooking the ranch is a hill where they could observe everything that was happening stood White Lightning and American Beauty side-by-side watching Pete treat the Colt.

The Colt eats from a bowl as Pete holds it. He puts the bowl down and the Colt continues to eat. Pete knows the two horses are watching him treat the colt. Pete saw that White

Lightning and the colt's mother were watching them so he decided to get out of the way and see what they would do. Pete rises, pets the Colt on the neck, and exits the corral. White Lightning and American Beauty continue to watch. Pete moves to the barn. He enters and hides from the view of the horses.

American Beauty decides to go to her son. White Lightning stays put. The Colt waits in the barn. American Beauty joins the Colt." Emery observed, "The mare moved to be near her colt just like any mother would." Pete exits the barn carrying a bowl of feed. He returns to the corral where the Colt and American Beauty are chewing on a bale of hay. He offers American Beauty a bowl of grain. At first she hesitates, and then she eats the grain. When the bowl is empty, Pete moves to the open corral gate and looks up the hill. White Lightning is still in the same place. Pete pushes the corral gate wide open and moves over by the fence next to the barn. He acts as if he is not interested in White Lightning. The great white horse paws the ground several times, and then heads down the hill. White Lightning walks cautiously as he heads for the corral."

Emery says, "White Lightning was a bit more skeptical. It took him a little while to make up his mind just what he wanted to do about it." White Lightning starts away from the ranch, stops and changes his mind. White Lightning turns and heads back toward the ranch.

White Lightning pauses at the open corral gate. He seems to be ready to enter, and then turns and runs back out to the open desert. Pete is in the barn waiting for White Lightning to join his son and American Beauty. Pete peeks around the corner, and shows his frustration that White Lightning decides not to enter by shaking his hat. White Lightning is in the semi-desert outside the ranch when he pauses, then turns. Pete, seeing this, makes a quick retreat back into hiding. White Lightning sticks his nose through the gate, and then cautiously moves to where American Beauty and the Colt are. He circles around, then joins them eating on the bale of hay." Emery, Sonny, and Mateo, all dismounted, are now near the roundup site. They take a break in the story.

BACK TO THE RIDGE ABOVE THE VALLEY Emery is looking at the herd and especially Black Fury, "He'd had an awful hard time out there in the wild country." Emery and Mateo take off their hats; all three sit down. "But when he found out that we wanted his family and didn't mean any harm to his family, he decided to stay. That's how I come to make the bargain with him. I promised him I'd let him run loose... (sweeping motion with his hat)... every day out all over the wild country if he'd promise not to run away. Cause, he's still a wild horse at heart" There's a pause. "So, Mateo, you see how it pays to keep your word with people." Mateo agrees, but asks, "Then, what happened to Black Fury?" Emery answers, "Well, Black Fury is still a wild horse"...White Lightning moves and goes to Emery..."and in this year's drive, they caught Black Fury again." Mateo gets excited and points, "Look! There's Black Fury now."

Four riders are in pursuit of a galloping Black Fury. One lasso after another is attached around Black Fury's neck. He puts up a fierce battle, finally he frees himself. The Riders charge after the stallion with lassos ready. He uses several evasive moves, circles a tree, and then finally gallops off...a free horse.

Emery shakes his head, "I wondered how they expect to hold that horse. (chuckle) Black Fury is loose again somewhere out on the range...in wild horse country there's another drama starting. White Lightning neighs as he sees Black Fury. Up on the edge of a cliff, Black Fury stands as if to show his magnificence. Numerous riders herd a large group of mustangs down a dry arroyo. The Riders have the situation under control as they move at a casual pace.

The mustangs are moving faster, kicking up dust. There are lots of YELPS and WHISTLING from the Riders. Despite the increase in speed, the horses are still under the control of the cowboys. White Lightning moves in and out of the herd as if he knows he is not subject to capture.

RIDGE ABOVE THE VALLEY

Mateo says,"Gee, Mister Emery, I'm sure glad White Lightning is safe now. Emery agrees, but says, "Oh, I don't think White Lightning would be scared because he's learned there's more contentment in an ordered, civilized life than running wild. You know, a lot of people could take a lesson from White Lightning because, after all"...Emery stands up and puts his hand on White Lightning's neck. "Because...he's a wild horse at heart, but he's satisfied. (to White

Lightning) Ain't 'cha White Lightning?" Emery puts his hat back on and moves away from White Lightning toward the roundup. Sonny and Mateo get up and follow Emery. White Lightning is satisfied to be guided by good and gentle influences. Emery, Sonny, and Mateo mount their horses and walk their animals down the hill. White Lightning neighs, shakes his head, and then follows them. "Look at that! Isn't that amazing?" The cowboys see one last panoramic view of running stallions as Emery, Sonny, Mateo, Tommy, and Old Hank continue downhill on their horses, White Lightning gallops up to follow them back to the ranch. "Let's go home. I didn't want to be a part of the mustang round-up, no how." Old Hank has joined them and leads the way back to the ranch.

- *Our goal is to protect America's wild horses and burros by stopping the federal government's systematic elimination of these national icons from our public lands. It's not too late to act to save the mustangs!*

THE END*

*ADDENDUM

INFORMATION TO HELP STUDY THE WILD MUSTANG SITUATION

Myths and Facts CONCERNING WILD HORSE AND BURRO MANAGEMENT

Contact: Tom Gorey, BLM Public Affairs (202-912-7420)

Updated as of August 7, 2015

Myth #1: A report issued in June 2013 by a 14-member research committee of the National Academy of Sciences (NAS) recommended that the BLM stop gathering wild horses and burros from Western public rangelands and let nature cull any excess herds.

Fact: *These characterizations are completely erroneous.* NAS's Board on

Agricultural and Natural Resources (BANR), which oversees the academy's natural resource studies, issued a special-edition newsletter in July that said: **"Some news accounts have incorrectly reported that the study found that the Bureau should stop gathers and 'let nature cull any excess herds.' In fact, the report recommends more intensive management of the horses and burros...."** BANR then cited

several management measures recommended by the report, including using scientifically rigorous methods to estimate the number of animals on the range; modeling the effects of management actions, such as the use of fertility-control treatments on mares and stallions and the removal of animals through gathers, on wild horse and burro health; and, following gathers, using the available one-year fertility-control vaccine (known as PZP) more widely and consistently to treat some mares.

The 383-page report itself, titled "Using Science to Improve the BLM Wild Horse and Burro Program: A Way Forward," makes it clear that to "let nature cull any excess herds" is not a viable option. The preface to the report, which does challenge the status quo of wild horse management, goes on to say in the very next sentence: **"It is equally evident that the consequences of simply letting horse populations, which increase at a mean annual rate approaching 20 percent, expand to the level of 'self-limitation'—bringing suffering and death due to disease, dehydration, and starvation accompanied by degradation of the land—are also unacceptable."**

Myth #2: It is the BLM's policy to sell or send wild horses to slaughter.

Fact: *This charge is absolutely false.* The Department of the Interior and the Bureau of Land Management care deeply about the well-being of wild horses, both on and off the range, and **it has been and remains the policy of the BLM not to sell or send wild horses or burros to slaughter.** Consequently, as noted in a report issued in October 2008, the Government Accountability Office found the BLM **not in compliance** with a December 2004 amendment (the so-called Burns Amendment to the 1971 Wild Free-Roaming Horses and Burros Act) that directs the Bureau to sell excess (unadopted or unsold) horses or burros **"without limitation"** to any willing buyer. For further information about the BLM's sales program, click here. To view a sample bill of sale, click here. The bill of sale, among other things, states that the buyer agrees not to process any of the sold horses or burros into commercial products, or to knowingly sell or transfer ownership to any person or organization whose intent is to commercially process the animals. On January 4, 2013, the BLM <u>announced</u> a policy stipulating that no more than four wild horses or burros may be bought by an individual or group within a six-month period without prior approval of the agency's Assistant Director for Renewable Resources and Planning.

Myth 3: Horses are held in crowded "holding pens."

Fact: *This assertion is false.* The BLM's short-term holding corrals provide ample space to horses, along with clean feed and water, while long-term holding pastures – large ranches located mainly in Kansas and Oklahoma – permit the horses to roam freely on approximately 289,000 acres of grassland.

Myth #4: Since 1971, the

BLM has illegally or improperly taken away more than 20 million acres set aside for wild horses and burros (from 53.8 million acres to 31.6 million acres).

Fact: *This claim is false.* **No specific amount of acreage was "set aside" for the exclusive use of wild horses and burros under the 1971 Wild Free-Roaming Horses and Burros Act.** The Act directed the BLM to determine the areas where horses and burros were found roaming and to manage them "in a manner that is designed to achieve and maintain a thriving natural ecological balance on the public lands." The law also stipulated in Section 1339 that "Nothing in this Act shall be construed to authorize the [Interior] Secretary to relocate wild free-roaming horses or burros to areas of the public lands where they do not presently exist." Of the 22.2 million acres no longer managed for wild horse and burro use:

6.7 million acres were never under BLM management.
Of the 15.5 million other acres of land under BLM   management:
48.6   percent (7,522,100   acres)   were intermingled   ("checkerboard")   land ownerships or areas where water was not owned or controlled by the BLM, which made management   infeasible;
13.5 percent (2,091,709 acres) were lands transferred out of the BLM's ownership to other agencies, both Federal and state through   legislation   or   exchange;
10.6 percent (1,645,758 acres) were lands where there were substantial conflicts with other resource values (such as the need to protect   habitat   for desert   tortoise);
9.7 percent (1,512,179 acres) were lands removed from wild horse and burro use through court decisions; urban expansion; highway   fencing   (causing   habitat fragmentation);   and   land   withdrawals;
9.6 percent (1,485,068 acres) were lands where no BLM animals were present at the time of the passage of the 1971 Act or places where all animals were claimed as private

property. These lands in future land-use plans will be subtracted from the BLM totals as they should never have been designated as lands where herds were found roaming; and

8.0 percent (1,240,894 acres) were lands where a critical habitat component (such as winter range) was missing, making the land unsuitable for wild horse and burro use, or areas that had too few animals to allow for effective management. (The percentages above were current as of July 25, 2011.)

Myth #5: The BLM is managing wild horse herds to extinction.

Fact: *This charge is patently false.* The 2015 on-range population of wild horses and burros (approximately 58,150) is greater than the number found roaming in 1971 (about 25,300). The BLM is seeking to achieve the Appropriate Management Level of 26,715 wild horses and burros on Western public rangelands, or about 31,500 fewer than the current West-wide population. The BLM also actively monitors the genetics of each herd by sending genetic samples to Dr. Gus Cothran at Texas A&M University. Dr. Cothran furnishes the BLM a report on every sample with recommendations for specific herds.

Myth #6: The BLM removes wild horses to make room for more cattle grazing on public rangelands.

Fact: *This claim is totally false.* The removal of wild horses and burros from public rangelands is carried out to ensure rangeland health, in accordance with land-use plans that are developed in an open, public process. These land-use plans are the means by which the BLM carries out its core mission, which is to manage the land for multiple uses while protecting the land's resources. **Livestock grazing on BLM-managed land has declined by 31 percent since 1971** (when Congress passed the Wild Free-Roaming Horses and Burros Act) -- from 12.1 million Animal Unit Months (AUMs or forage units) to 8.3 million AUMs in 2014.

Myth #7: The BLM lacks the legal authority to gather animals from overpopulated herds or to use helicopters in doing so.

Fact: *This assertion is false.* Section 1333 of the 1971 Wild Free-Roaming Horses and Burros Act mandates that once the Interior Secretary "determines...on the basis of all information currently available to him, that an overpopulation exists on a given area of the public lands and that action is necessary to remove excess animals, **he shall immediately remove excess animals from the range so as to achieve appropriate management levels.**" Section 1338 of the law authorizes the BLM's use of helicopters and motorized vehicles in its management of wild horses and burros.

Myth #8: Gathers of wild horses by helicopter are inhumane.

Fact: *This claim is false.* The BLM's helicopter-assisted gathers are conducted humanely, as affirmed by three recent independent reports (see below), and have proven to be more humane, effective, and efficient than other types of gather methods when large numbers of animals need to be removed over wide areas or rugged terrain. Helicopters start the horses moving in the right direction and then back off sometimes one-quarter to one-half mile from the animals to let them travel at their own pace; horses are moved at a more rapid pace when they need to be turned or as they reach the entrance to the capture site. Helicopter pilots are better able to keep mares and foals together than horseback riders; pilots can also more effectively move the animals around such barriers as deep ravines, fences, or roads.

In Fiscal Year 2014, out of 1,863 wild horses and burros removed, a total of 18 animals, or approximately one percent (0.97 percent), died or were euthanized during gather operations; of those 18, nine animals, or about one-half of one percent (0.48 percent) of the removed animals, died or were euthanized because of acute injuries. **Acute injury deaths** include all animals that died or were euthanized because of acute injuries, such as spinal cord or head injuries, fractured limbs, or other severe injuries that occurred during gathers. **Total deaths** include all animals that died or were euthanized for any reason during gathers, including acute or sudden injuries or illnesses, as well as chronic or pre-existing conditions that required euthanasia (such as limb deformities, lameness, and poor body condition).

Two reports issued in the fall of 2010 (one by four independent, credentialed equine professionals and one by the Interior Department's Office of Inspector General), plus another report released in 2011 by the American

Association of Equine (Veterinary) Practitioners, found -- without any ideological or political bias -- that the BLM's gathers of wild horses are conducted in a humane manner. The Inspector General determined that the BLM's gathers are "justified" and reported that the agency "is doing its best to perform a very difficult job."

Myth #9: If left alone, wild horses will automatically balance their reproduction rate with rangeland conditions.

Fact: There were an estimated 25,300 wild horses and burros in 1971, and those numbers rose to a peak of more than 60,000 before the BLM was authorized and able to effectively use helicopters for gathers. If left unchecked, Mother Nature would regulate the wild horse and burro population through the classic boom-and-bust cycle, where the population increases dramatically, food becomes scarce, and the population crashes through starvation or dehydration.

Myth #10: The BLM overestimates the number of wild horses and burros on the range.

Fact: *This assertion is false.* In its June

2013 report ("Using Science to Improve the BLM Wild Horse and Burro Program: A Way Forward"), the National Academy of Sciences (NAS) concluded that the BLM's "direct count" aerial survey method has resulted in population undercounts of 20 percent to 30 percent because it does not account for undetected animals. To more accurately estimate population size, the BLM applied the U.S. Geological Survey (USGS) population survey methods in 2014, consisting of the use of "simultaneous double-count" and "photographic mark-resight" methods commonly used to survey wildlife populations. The BLM will continue to survey one-third of all 179 Herd Management Areas annually, on a rolling basis, using the USGS methods, as recommended by NAS.

Myth #11: The Government Accountability Office, in a report issued in October 2008, found that the BLM has been mismanaging the Wild Horse and Burro Program.

Fact: *This claim is completely false.* The GAO made no such finding. The full report can be accessed here:http://www.gao.gov/new.items/d0977.pdf

Myth #12: Wild horses are native to the

United States.

Fact: *This claim is false.* The disappearance of the horse from the Western Hemisphere for 10,000 years supports the position that today's American wild horses should not be considered "native." American wild horses are descended from domestic horses, some of which were brought over by European explorers in the late 15th and 16th centuries, plus others that were released or escaped captivity in modern times. Over this 500-year period, these horses (and burros) have adapted successfully to the Western range. Regardless of the debate over whether these animals are native or non-native, the BLM manages horses and burros on public lands according to the provisions of the 1971 Wild Free-Roaming Horses and Burros Act, which describes the animals as "wild" rather than feral.

Myth #13: Two million wild horses roamed the United States in the late 1800s/early 1900s.

Fact: *This figure has no scientific basis.* In a book titled *The Mustangs* (1952) by J. Frank Dobie, the historian noted that no scientific estimate of wild horse numbers was made in the 19th century or early 20th century. He went on to write: "All guessed numbers are mournful to history. My own **guess** is that **at no time** were there more than a million mustangs in Texas and no more than a million others scattered over the remainder of the West." (Emphasis added.) Mr. Dobie's admitted "guess" of no more than two million mustangs has over the years been transformed into an asserted or assumed "fact" that two million mustangs actually roamed America in the late 1800s/early 1900s. When Congress assigned the BLM (and the U.S. Forest Service) to manage wild horses and burros in 1971 -- through passage of the Wild Free-Roaming Horses and Burros Act -- the BLM's population survey methods indicated a population of 17,300 wild horses and 8,045 burros (=25,345 total), as compared to the 2015 estimated population of 47,329 horses and 10,821 burros (=58,150 total).

Myth #14: Under the 1971 Wild Free-Roaming Horses and Burros Act, BLM-administered public lands where wild horses and burros were found roaming in 1971 are to be managed "principally but not necessarily exclusively" for the welfare of these animals.

Fact: The law's language stating that public lands where wild horses and burros were found roaming in 1971 are to be managed "principally but not necessarily exclusively" for the welfare of these animals relates to the Interior Secretary's power to "designate and maintain **specific ranges** on public lands as sanctuaries for their protection and preservation" -- which are, thus far, the Pryor Mountain Wild Horse Range (in Montana and Wyoming), the Nevada Wild Horse Range (located within the north central portion of Nellis Air Force Range), the Little Book Cliffs Wild Horse Range (in Colorado), and the Marietta Wild Burro Range (in Nevada). The "principally but not necessarily exclusively" language applies to **specific Wild Horse Ranges**, not to Herd Management Areas in general. The Code of Federal Regulations (43 CFR, Subpart 4710.3-2) states: "Herd management areas **may also be designated as wild horse or burro ranges** to be managed principally, but not necessarily exclusively, for wild horse or burro herds."

Myth #15: The Code of Federal Regulations (43 CFR) specifies that the BLM is to allocate forage to wild horses and burros in an amount "comparable" to that allocated to wildlife and cattle.

Fact: The Code of Federal Regulations (43

CFR, Subpart 4700.0-6) states that "Wild horses and burros **shall be considered comparably with other resource values** in the formulation of land use plans." This regulation means that in its development of land-use plans, the BLM will consider wild horses and burros in a manner similar to the way it treats other resource values (e.g., cultural, historic, wildlife, and scenic, as distinguished from authorized commercial land uses, such as livestock grazing or timber harvesting).